W9-AHE-171

Introduction

A Pocket Full of Posies is based on a collection of writings authored by my mom, Martha Benedict, which were published in *The Santa Cruz Connection* from 2001 to 2004. *The Connection* featured local businesses and health practitioners with a focus on alternative healing. She was invited to contribute her thoughts on the healing process while talking about the herbal products she developed in her acupuncture practice. *Posie,* originally produced in limited quantities, has been modified and updated for this printing.

The articles highlight specific beliefs of hers while providing sage advice about lifestyle choices and showcasing the herbal products developed by her. As herbal popularity and use has exploded in the last decades, the need for reliable, high-quality herbal products that have withstood the rigors of clinical practice has increased.

She combined several herbal traditions including Chinese, American Indian, and European to develop formulas for patients with specific needs. Many of the herbs used in her formulas are still grown without pesticides in the BHP garden and are harvested and processed by hand using time-tested methods. The herbal products, when possible, are made from whole plants that are prepared by infusion, decoction or extraction in water, alcohol, vinegar, extra virgin olive oil or other oils appropriate for its application. Honey and beeswax from our bees are also used.

My mom's legacy was her commitment to healing. She studied and used herbs for more than forty years. She had a Master's

Degree from Stanford University School of Medicine, worked to legalize acupuncture in California and received one of the first licenses granted in the state; and co-founded and taught at one of the first oriental medical colleges, the American College of Traditional Chinese Medicine, in San Francisco. My mom taught classes at a number of additional institutions and for Chinese medical and herbal professional groups nationwide. She studied various healing philosophies all over the world, embracing and incorporating a wide variety of beliefs into her practice.

Additionally, she formulated herbs and taught classes for the nutraceutical company, Metagenics. She wrote numerous workbooks, teaching tapes and articles, and was a radio host showcasing herbs and alternative medicine. For years she maintained an acupuncture practice in Santa Cruz, CA, specializing in women's health, elder concerns, facial acupuncture and weight management.

In many ways, her thinking about health and the body was ahead of its time. She believed that it was crucial to address the fundamental building blocks of health in order to treat and heal the body. In order to do that, we need to focus on a quality diet, regular exercise, getting adequate sleep, and dealing with our emotional issues. She believed, and science has since born out, that most health issues can be addressed at such a fundamental level.

In the 2.5 years since her passing, we have endeavored to keep her herbal legacy alive. With the help of key members of my mom's community, we have been able to continue the production of her unique herbal formulas and in our small way, continue to provide her healing knowledge to the public.

A Pocket Full of Posies

A Collection of Herbal Wisdom

By Martha Benedict

Editors:

Maartje Eagle

David W Klemp

RDP BOOKS

Santa Cruz, CA 95060

COPYRIGHT ©2004, 2006, 2010, 2015 Martha Benedict, Benedictine Healing Products LLC.

All rights reserved. No part of this book may be reproduced in any form or by any means without prior written consent of the Publisher.

Cover Illustration by Caroline Klemp
Copyright ©2004 Caroline Klemp. All Rights Reserved.

Edited by Maartje Eagle and David W Klemp

Revised Edition, September, 2015

ISBN10: 1518825346

ISBN13: 9781518825347

Printed in the United States of America

Maartje Eagle, Editor

Table of Contents

Herbs Work

Why are people still using herbs? Because they are effective. Because they are safe. Because they work.

A few years ago, a Neolithic man was found frozen in the Italian-Swiss Alps. He carried a pouch containing plants such as comfrey, chamomile and feverfew: a medicine pouch. Identical herbs are used today in many households all over the world.

Historically, herbs have surfaced and resurfaced in popularity over the centuries. The pursuit and commerce in culinary herbs has been an important impetus for global exploration. The use of medicinal herbs and who could control their use is an historical saga wherein many people died. In Europe, women were burned as witches for using herbs. It was not until Henry VIII wrote a law protecting the use of herbs by herbalists that this witch-hunting stopped.

Until today, this part of British Common Law is our law except where local statute overrides. There have been several attempts to take herbs out of the hands of the public and to put them under control of medical bureaucracy. We are currently witnessing another such attempt. There has been powerful lobbying to have herbs put under FDA control to protect the public against unscrupulous businesses abusing a few herbs. I believe the lawbreakers putting dangerous products on the market ought to be stopped, and there are already plenty of existing laws on the books to do so.

Taking away public access to all herbs doesn't seem like a reasonable response. It strikes me that the powers-that-be have tipped their hand. This attempt smacks at overt suppression and control—not as much for public safety, but to ensure economic entitlement for a small minority. We have recently quietly given up so many of our basic freedoms; I am not willing to give up another one.

Herbs are safe. If you tally the percentage of side effects experienced by people using herbs and the percentage of the side effects from standard medical drugs and procedures, it puts the issue in perspective. The few incidents of side effects with herbs don't begin to compare to the lists of side effects generated by pharmaceuticals. Herbs help mitigate unpleasant symptoms. People wouldn't have continued to use the same herbs for centuries if they didn't work.

I encourage readers to use herbs instead of prescription drugs whenever possible. Learn what they look like and what they are used for. There are many good herb teachers in our community like Jeanine Pollak and Darren Huckle at the American School of Herbalism. There are several small local herb companies like my own that provide excellent herbal formulas when you cannot make your own. Many herbs are the weeds that are found in our yards, empty lots, and along pathways. Grow them yourself or purchase organically grown plants. Use the unhybridized, old fashioned, "officinalis" form of the plant. Harvest them where the soil is clean and they haven't been exposed to car exhaust or other pollutants. These herbs have been around since Neolithic man.

"Herbs work... they are effective, safe, and work."

The Cost of Herbs

Using herbs in your daily activities is one of the most cost-effective ways of staying healthy. Consider the difference in cost between using herbs and the cost of many prescriptions from pharmaceutical companies. First consider using herbs preventively in your daily life. They can be added to beverages and as ingredients and seasonings in meals. Herbs are nutrient dense and include antioxidants, anti-microbial and anti-cancer agents—and they make your food taste better! For example, triple mint tea—peppermint, spearmint, and lemon balm (really a mint) with lemon on a hot day quenches thirst and has a pleasing flavor. Adding fennel seeds to a spaghetti sauce increases digestibility and taste.

It is simple to grow your own herbs in an herb box outside, or purchase herbs at any grocery store. One summer my herb garden consisted of one basil plant on my dining room table. I used basil to season a mineral-rich tonic beverage. Most people would agree that adding basil to salads, dressings, and vegetable-entrée dishes is delicious and adds a bitter flavor to a salad similar to endive or arugula.

Medicinal herbs are where you can often see a big difference in cost between prescription medicines and herbal preparations that may be appropriate for your needs. When you start using herbs, have an herbalist help find the best remedy for your care. However, once you know your body and have experience working with herbal remedies, many people have learned just how far **herbs can help in assisting them feel better and keeping down medical costs.**

3

Herbs for Back to School

Summer is over and kids are back in school. Providing nutritious and appealing school lunches of organic food (protein, quality oils, veggies and fruit) is an important way to keep kids healthy. This is a cornerstone of the prevention of illness.

If you observe your child coming home in the evenings tired with dark circles under their eyes, or being unusually irritable, act before the first sneeze. One of the first principles in traditional Chinese medicine to reverse the common cold (viral) is to *relieve the surface*, or induce perspiration. This is simple to do with hot soup, hot tea, a hot bath or shower, or light exercising until perspiration appears. Vitamin C and L. acidophilus are also useful. **Anti-X**, a decoction of anti-viral herbs, focuses on the upper-respiratory system and is appropriate for all stages and symptoms of cold and flu including, sneezing, muscle aches, sinus involvement, headaches, and mucus. If your child has a tendency toward sore throats, you may make a cup of **Traditional Medicinals' Throat Coat** tea or use **Chinese Cold & Flu**. For coughing, hot water with lemon and honey, together with **Elderberry Plus** is pleasant and very soothing. If the infection progresses and gets to the bronchi or lungs, **Deep Lung** is helpful. **Deep Lung 3 in 1** combines **Anti-X, Chinese Cold & Flu,** and **Deep Lung** for convenient treatment of cold and flu symptoms. Also, **Sniffles for Kids** is a modified **Deep Lung 3 in 1** specifically for children.

In the Fall, it is hard to anticipate the weather so it is especially important to dress in layers. Have your children wear a turtleneck and hooded jacket for early and late in the day and

4

a short sleeved tee shirt underneath for midday heat. Now if you could just get your kids to remember not to leave their jacket at school!

When making school lunches, creativity, enthusiasm, variety, and child participation in the decision-making and preparation process will pay off. Drinks are the biggest source of sugar in lunches. A bottle of water is the best, but at the very least, make sure you are not buying one that says water, sugar, concentrate.

Another guideline that worked in our family for sandwiches is the 'five veggie rule'. That means I needed to add at least 5 vegetables to the sandwich. For example, your child may like lettuce, sprouts, mashed avocado (in place of mayo), or blending a variety of greens into the bread spread such as cilantro, basil, parsley, avocado, or dill, and adding a little yogurt or mayo to the green mix. Mincing colored peppers, olives, jicama, pickles, radish, and thinly sliced cucumbers or even steamed veggies also work well to flavor the sandwich.

Making homemade organic beef, turkey, or salmon jerky is a way to increase your child's participation and is easy and inexpensive. Bags of mixed raw or lightly toasted nuts, coconut strips, currants, raisins, and a variety of seeds can be easily made at home and are a healthful alternative to a bag of chips. Fresh fruit such as a kiwi, apple, pear or tangerine, whole or cut into pieces quenches thirst and satisfies the sweet tooth.

"Creativity, enthusiasm, variety, and kid participation in the decision-making and preparation process will pay off."

Preparation for the Cold-Flu Season

Everyone is exposed to cold and flu germs, especially as the weather changes. It is possible to avoid sick days with a little preparation. Here are a few old wives tales that have been corroborated by modern science.

According to Chinese Medicinal theory, it is just as important to dress right as well as eat right. Dress in layers and protect your head and neck from wind chill. Make a hearty **chicken soup** and freeze it in advance for a quick meal later. Prepare hot soups that include **ginger, onions,** and **garlic.** Use **vitamin C**, **L. acidophilus**, and **fish liver oil**. Prepare hot tea with **lemons, limes, slippery elm,** and **mint.** Find ways to reduce stress— take a walk, exercise, go hot-tubbing, have a massage, or get some acupuncture.

Go to bed earlier than usual. Traditional Chinese medical theory substantiated by recent scientific information indicates that cellular repair occurs during sleep especially the hours before midnight. Focus the power of your mind on the important considerations in your life. It is a very powerful tool to support a healthy body.

If you use herbs, create a Care Kit from the following formulas. By having the correct herbs on hand to use immediately, you will be more likely to use them early in the development of the cold-flu when they can be most effective.

Keep **Chinese Cold and Flu,** or **Echinacea** for the first sneeze. To enhance immunity, consider **Immunity Plus, Reishi, Nettles,** and **Herbal Mineral Tonic.** If there are sinus symptoms, use **Anti-X** or **Bi Yan Pian.** If necessary you may include **Feverfew** for headaches. For cough and copious mucous, **Elderberry Plus** is effective**.**

For a viral (flu) infection, **Calendula, Olive, Usnea,** and **Anti-X** may be helpful**.** For sore throats, swollen glands, and ear infections, take **Chinese Cold and Flu** or **Phytolacca** and rub **Lymph Oil** on neck and near ear to reduce pain and inflammation.

For ear pressure or discomfort drop warmed **Chinese Ear Oil** into the ear canal and stuff the ear with cotton. Be careful and make sure it isn't too hot and because it stains. **Mullein Flower Oil** is useful in the recovery period. Use **Lymph Oil** on the neck and throat and near ears.

Two blends useful for people who get frequent or serious respiratory infections are **Deep Lung** and **Anti-X**. Use **Anti-X** for sinus involvement when the head is runny or stuffy. **Deep Lung** is best when the infection drops below the throat into the chest. Both are safe to use with children.

To correct constipation, use **Butternut Bark Plus**, which includes anise to warm the stomach and butternut to cool the intestine. For joint and muscle aches and that *done in* feeling, after a soak in a tub or a long hot shower, rub **Arnica Oil** into the affected area.

Take good care of yourself through rest, exercise, diet, and healthy mental activities. Being prepared is cost effective and makes good sense.

Cold and Flu Season Recommendations

Cold and flu season makes headlines every year, especially when new forms of the virus appear. Here are some guidelines from Benedictine Healing Products for mitigating the effects.

Rest: It's a verb! It is important to plan and make time for adequate rest just as you plan to exercise or go out to dinner and a movie. Going to bed a few minutes early, sitting once or twice a day with your feet up and eyes closed–even for 5 minutes—does make a difference. Taking a nap or staying in bed with a good book or DVD is healthy when feeling under the weather.

Consume Warm Fluids: Drinking warm herbal teas and preparing soups with onions, garlic, and veggies in bone broth; chicken soup, egg drop soup, miso, consume or strong veggie broth hits the spot. Not only are they delicious, but they're good for you too. Hold a bowl of broth in your hands and inhale the hot aromas.

Herbs to induce sweating are especially good for the first stage of infection. These include peppermint, spearmint, ginger, and chamomile. Add a pinch of cayenne to enhance therapeutic value.

For cough, slippery elm with honey, or lemon and honey (and ½ tsp. brandy) is appealing.

Vitamin C complex: Taking vitamin C is no longer controversial as it once was when Linus Pauling first suggested it in the 1960's. There are several ways to get the needed dose of vitamin C. My favorites, depending upon the need, are consuming fresh fruits and veggies, and a special form of degraded vitamin C that bypasses the intestinal system and stays in the intestinal tract a couple of days instead of 4 hours before being eliminated. **Metagenics Ultra Potent C** is a high quality source of this form of vitamin C.

Vitamin A: Take large amounts for 3 days to stimulate the immune system.

Vitamin D₃: For most people, consume 2000 IU in the short term to support the immune system.

Gentle Movement and Joint Articulation: A short walk, a few minutes of yoga stretching or qigong breathing, even splashing in a hot tub for movement of the joints and articulation of the body is helpful to avoid getting sick. There is a belief in Chinese thought that "evils" (virus and bacteria) lurk near the joints so gentle movement allows them to be thrust from their hiding places where the blood constituents can eliminate them efficiently.

A **Hot Shower** or **Hot Salt Bath** with Epsom salt or sea salt: This can induce sweating, thereby reducing toxic lymphatic waste.

L. acidophilus: Increase the use of intestinal flora products such as Lactobacillus acidophilus to enhance the body's ability to cleanse the intestine. I recommend 15-450 billion per dose.

Herbal Recommendations: General herbal recommendations include stocking up on **Chinese Cold & Flu**, and **Anti-X**. Keep on hand using very early in the cycle of the illness if the symptoms are present in the throat or head.

9

If an individual has a pattern of lung weakness, include **Deep Lung** as well. **Deep Lung 3 in 1** is a cost-effective source of these three remedies.

Progression of Colds and Flu

These attacks on our immune system occur in three stages.

In **stage 1**, the cold enters the body via the upper respiratory tracts as a virus. In Traditional Chinese Medicine the thought is that you need to protect the back of the head, neck, and chest for *wind*. Symptoms include achy muscles, stuffy head and nose, headache, sore throat, low grade fever, cough, clear or colored phlegm or mucous, and a probable change in bowel activity. This is obviously the best stage to prevent the illness with home remedies and herbs.

If the cold progresses to **stage 2** it has progressed to include a bacterial response to the initial viral invasion and this is when you will feel really sick. If you're inclined to use western medicine, this is the stage to use it. The symptoms become worse and more interior, such as a really sore throat with swollen glands, ear ache, movement and into the bronchi or lungs with lots of highly colored mucus from sinuses and chest.

Stage 3 is the final stage of infection where the virus returns to the sinuses before resolving and completing its cycle.

Useful BHP Products:

Deep Lung 3 in 1: A blend of **Anti-X, Chinese Cold & Flu,** and **Deep Lung**. Keep on hand for the whole family. Add additional amounts of component formulas as necessary.

Anti-X: All herbs are antiviral and additionally some are antibacterial. It is useful in stage 1, 2, and 3.

Chinese Cold & Flu: This formula is especially useful for sore throat, lymph, and to keep the liver open in dealing with infection. Evodia has been added to slightly warm the stomach as the other three herbs are considered very cold and would compromise the digestive system. Adding this fourth herb allows the formula to be used with more confidence by the young, pregnant and nursing mothers, as well as the elderly, and infirm.

Deep Lung: This formula is most useful in stage 2 after or 18 hours when the infection may have descended into the bronchi or lower, or moved into the bacterial stage.

Elderberry Plus: This formula contains no sugar, but relies on a thick concentration of the berries themselves. It is useful for coughing as well as a tonic for the lungs, and immunity. Because it is sweet, it is well received by young children.

Astragalus: This is best applied in stage 3 and in the re-cooperative stages until the natural energy (chi) has returned. It is especially useful in cold and wet lung conditions. Do not use it for a dry lung condition or if it appears to increase coughing.

Immunity Plus: A comprehensive herbal immune tonic best used for 3 weeks before expected exposure to infection or throughout the entire season by susceptible patients.

Olive: This is a strong antimicrobial and antiviral that many find useful when experiencing viral eruptions, such as herpes.

Usnea: This is another strong antimicrobial many find useful when experiencing respiratory and urinary infections.

Chinese Ear Oil: This is an effective topical application for ear pain. NOTE: It stains clothing and needs to be stored in the refrigerator when not in use. It must be heated to just slightly warmer than body temperature before putting 1 to 3 eye droppers full in the ear canal. Plug the canal with a big wad of cotton to contain the oil.

Mullein Ear Oil: This topical oil is useful after the active ear infection if over, but it is still necessary to use something to continue treating the ear for another week. [See Chinese Ear Oil for instructions.]

Lymph Oil: This topical oil is applied in lymph rich areas such as the neck or groin area to facilitate the movement of overburdened lymph glands in the removal of infection waste material. I use it extensively for both children and adults with ear aches and swollen throat glands. It has also been helpful for children with chronic ear infections.

Echinacea: This is a mild lymph mover useful in fighting infection.

Phytolacca: This is a strong lymph mover useful in fighting sore throats and infection. It is extremely important not to exceed dose recommendations as it may have a toxic effect.

Breathe Easier: An antimicrobial solution with phenolated iodine in an Irish moss extract with organic borates that is used topically to soothe and shrink swollen membranes of nose and throat. It stings only when applied to inflamed tissue, but not healthy tissue.

Immunity

Everyone wants a magic bullet to enhance their immune system. According to ancient Chinese medicinal theory, immunity is a protective Yang energy of the body. It is accurate to say that **Ginseng**, **Reishi**, **Eleutherococcus**, or **Cordyceps** are herbs that build immunity. Herbs that enjoy this reputation do so because they enhance the body's ability to perform its functions in a more optimal way.

Every cell, organ, and system, when functioning at an optimal level and in harmony with its environment, optimizes immunity. It is necessary to understand how an individual maintains and supports life force (chi) to put this into perspective.

The stomach contributes to immunity by producing sufficient gastric secretions in order to completely digest its contents as well as destroy most pathogens reaching the stomach. The lungs enhance immunity when filled and refilled with deep breaths of fresh clean air. The large intestine contributes to immunity by eliminating food waste once or twice a day. The kidneys filter the blood, removing waste. The same goes for the liver. The gallbladder stores bile and dumps it in response to food consumed. It alkalinizes the gut, destroys more pathogens, and stimulates peristalsis that in turn increases bowel elimination. The heart in Chinese theory not only pumps blood, but also controls metabolism, intelligence and integrity; all of which help the individual to make healthy decisions.

Each of us can learn what we need to provide our body for it to perform optimally. For example, one patient recently contracted a bladder infection. After appropriate lab work, we started acupuncture and an herbal regime. Using a low dose of **Kidney Care, L. Acidophilus,** and **unsweetened cranberry juice**, her symptoms reversed very quickly. I saw her three days after she started this program. The pain and infection were resolved, her mood cheerful, and even her skin was clearer. She confided that she had stopped drinking coffee, was going to bed earlier, drinking more water, eating more cooked vegetables, didn't forget to eat protein, and stopped partying so hard. This is an example of how what we do affects how we function.

Each person who is looking to reinforce immunity needs to re-examine lifestyle choices and honestly assess the ones that are not supporting their most optimum experience of health, wealth, and happiness. Some of the specific herbs you may wish to include in your daily or weekly pattern include: **Reishi, Cordyceps** and other mushrooms, **Eleutherococcus, Astragalus, Ashwagandha, Foti, Nettles, Cat's Claw, Ginkgo** and **Rhodiola Rosea.** Some Benedictine Healing Product formulas that blend multiple immune supportive herbs that are worth checking out are: **Immunity Plus, Mega Ginseng, Herbal Minerals, Holiday Bitters, No Burp, Gum Protect,** and **Tummy Ease.**

"Every cell, organ, and system, when functioning at an optimal level and in harmony with its environment, optimizes immunity."

Protein: The Building Block of Life

Protein is back in vogue again after having taken its turn at the back of the bus for the last thirty years. Part of its fall from favor may have had to do with the unavailability of natural (no hormone, no antibiotics) animal products. Part may have had to do with the poorly understood chemistry of body metabolism, and part may have to do with the gung-ho extremist American attitude that if one is good, two is better, or in this case, if excess (meat) is bad for you, absence (of meat) must be good.

Now some of these issues have been addressed. In our community we have several meat counters that specialize in natural and free-range grass-fed organic meat sources - Staff of Life, New Leaf, Shoppers Corner, Trader Joe's and Corralitos Meats. Other stores carry at the minimum, natural poultry. Perhaps the consumer is beginning to become aware of some of the health consequences of continual exposure to antibiotics and hormones in food sources. There is published evidence that antibiotic exposure is carried over into our bodies and plays a part in antibiotic resistance if ever there is a real need to use them.

As a practitioner of Chinese medicine for over forty years, I've learned I cannot be successful in assisting a woman balance her hormone profile if she consumes animal protein pumped with hormones. Hormones are given to animals just before going to market to enhance weight gain and therefore company profits.

16

Another well-documented source of information is a cookbook by Sally Fallon, called _Nourishing Traditions_. Even if the recipes do not appeal to you, the well-researched information about the role and importance of protein and fats in our diet is invaluable. There is no marketing hype or facts taken out of context. If I had an altar to dietary and health common sense, Sally would be at the center of it!

One of the reasons I appreciate Sally's book so much is because it documents and explains in modern language my understanding of the importance of protein in Chinese medical food theory.

Protein is the building block of cell structure, DNA, the Chi, life force, kidney energy, and ancestral energy–all ways of saying similar things. Individuals differ in the amount and timing of their protein needs. A monk chanting and praying six hours a day who does not till his own rice field does not have the same protein requirements as a nursing mother of three. Specific needs and preferences can certainly be accommodated. In general, I find small amounts of a wide variety of animal protein, one to three ounces, two to four times per day, is the way to go. Vegetarians need to be four times more vigilant to ensure appropriate quantity and variety.

Grains and legumes soaked for a day and a half contain far more protein and a more inclusive amino acid profile than unsoaked grains. The USDA (United States Department of Agriculture) publishes, for example, that rice, a 10%, 8 amino acid profile grain, becomes a 60%, 16 amino acid grain after 48 hours of soaking. It also takes a lot less time and fuel to cook soaked grains. Mixing different soaked grains and legumes and adding them to soups, salads, and different dishes is invaluable. Tofu and other soy products are useful for some people, but many are allergic or cannot digest soy very easily. If you find soy a useful protein source, the label needs to read "non-GMO and organic".

Bee pollen, clabbered dairy products such as buttermilk, yogurt, kefir and eggs from a variety of chickens, ducks, quail and turkeys, as well as fish eggs (caviar) have been acceptable to some vegetarians over the years. For those whose protein preference includes meat, variety is just as important. Red meat (lamb, beef, and pork) nourishes the body in different ways than white meat (chicken, turkey). Fish with scales that swim near the top of the waterline (salmon, sardines, anchovies, sea bass, halibut, snapper, herring, mackerel) are nutrient dense and should be included as well as more popular bottom feeders (prawns, scallops, crab, lobster). It is important when eating animal protein to eat vegetables at the same time to avoid any pitfalls of excess protein.

Alas, there must be a solution for the attitude of extremism, but with the exception of education, I haven't found it.

Debunking the Myths about Fats and Oils

The American diet is characterized by an excess of pro-inflammatory processed omega 6 oils and a dearth of anti-inflammatory omega 3 oils due to our reliance on highly heated and refined vegetable oils. In fact, most of our oils come from the industrial waste of soy, cottonseed, and corn. The processing of vegetable oils at high heat (230 degrees or more) destroys the protective double and triple chemical bonds that are characteristic of good oils, thus increasing the free radicals that ravage our blood vessels and cause harm.

Another cultural myth is that animal fat is bad, leading to our cultural avoidance of animal oils, including fish. There are many fats in animal products that are necessary for healthy body function. When there is an excess ratio of omega 6 to omega 3 oils, there can be interference with the enzymes that change the long chain highly unsaturated fatty acids, which are the precursors of healthy prostaglandins that in turn, direct many cell processes. The excess of omega 6's to omega 3's may also exist in some plant-sourced oils. This unfortunate situation may lead to hypertension, irritation of the digestive system, inflammation, depressed immunity, weight gain, sterility, and cancer.

Oils that are highly heated in their processing include hydrogenated oils, partially hydrogenated oils (worse), pasteurized oils (high heat), and ultra-pasteurized oils (even higher heat). The newest chemical process to avoid is "interesterification" of oils where liquid oils can be transformed into solids. If that weren't bad enough, toxic chemicals are used in the refining processes. Although there is a process to remove the chemical extracting agent, there are legally allowed residues of these chemicals. For example, in the hydrogenation process used to make margarine and vegetable shortening, nickel oxide must be used and is responsible for changing the naturally occurring healthy "cis" formation of a chemical bond into an unhealthy "trans" form of that bond. For more almost forty years we have known that this "trans" form of the bond is implicated in arterial and cardiovascular disease.

Solvents used in the extraction and processing of oils include hexane, benzene, gasoline, ethyl ether, carbon disulfide, toluene, carbon tetrachloride, and methylene chloride - all legally allowed toxic substances that leave legally allowed residues in the oil.

Homogenization, the process of breaking large dairy fats into small ones that stay suspended in milk, allows the fats to become prone to oxidation and rancidity. This free radical formation has been implicated in hastening the aging of the skin and body organs, auto-immune diseases such as arthritis, cataracts, Parkinson's, Lou Gehrig disease, and Alzheimers' disease.

It is important to be discriminating about oils. You should spend the largest percentage of your food dollar on excellent quality oils. Ask questions in the supermarkets and restaurants. Sound like heresy? It's not. It's science and it's our genetics, our body chemistry and our health.

"Another cultural myth is that animal fat is bad."

Oils and fats heated at high temperatures, under great pressure, and using toxic solvents in the manufacturing process damages chemical bonds that create serious consequences. Over-heated oils promote free radical damage and inflammation to the blood vessels and other body tissue. When this occurs the body produces a substance to repair the damage: cholesterol. Cholesterol is the body's answer to oxidative stress and inflammation. Cholesterol acts as an antioxidant. Additionally, cholesterol is important in many other body functions. It is a precursor to vitamin D, bile, adrenaline, estrogen, progesterone, as well as steroids that protect against heart disease and cancer. Cholesterol is a receptor for serotonin in the brain. We absorb about one third of the cholesterol we ingest while the rest of our cholesterol is manufactured by our body.

Some of the common sources of heat-damaged oils that I recommend you avoid include powdered milk, pasteurized milk, ultra-pasteurized milk, homogenized milk, and powdered eggs. Hydrogenated oils such as margarine and vegetable shortening are particularly offensive. Although the evidence is not yet conclusive about GMO (gene-modified organism) canola oil, I recommend avoiding it until we know more.

Fats and oils have been given a bum rap. The truth is we need a variety of oils: saturated and unsaturated, mono-unsaturated, polyunsaturated, short, medium, long and extra-long chain fatty acids. We need omega 3's and omega 6's. Translated into English, this means coconut oil and butter give you energy immediately and 15% of the fat structures in these oils do not store in our fat cells, a fact to keep in mind when wanting to increase energy or lose weight. We all know that monounsaturated fat (oleic) such as extra-virgin olive oil is very good for us. Double unsaturated linoleic acid or omega 6 is most useful in building the brain and nervous system, especially for infants. Triple unsaturated linolenic acid or omega 3 found in fish and flaxseed oil is even more useful. Each of these fats and oils participates in the body in different ways.

What oils do I recommend? Non-GMO. Organic. Cold-pressed. 100% extra-virgin. Be vigilant in your pursuit of excellent quality oils. Be prepared to pay for them. Quality oils should be used in our foods as well as in the oils we put on our body, or allowed to come in contact with our skin. Even the Essential Oils we inhale should come from excellent non-chemical sources. Think about that the next time you are purchasing soap, bath oils, mood oils, cosmetics, or dry skin oil. I strongly recommend small amounts of many of the following high quality oils: 100% extra-virgin olive oil (plain olive oil is not pure enough), coconut oil, palm oil, nut oils, seed oils, grape seed oil, rice bran oil, ghee, fish oils, peanut, walnut, sesame, unpasteurized cream and butter, grass-fed animal fat and lard, nitrite-free bacon, goose and duck fat, runny egg yolks from organically fed cage-free hens, and fish roe.

"Cholesterol acts as an anti-oxidant."

"Cholesterol is a precursor to Vitamin D."

"Cholesterol is a receptor for serotonin in the brain."

Blood Sugar Balance

Keeping blood sugar levels stable can be a challenge. We all are aware that eating well—not skipping meals, getting plenty of protein, high quality oils, abundant fresh fruits and veggies—is the way to go. Implementing what we know takes dedication.

There is abundant research that correlates blood sugar levels with mood, ability to focus, mental acuity, and performance. When blood sugar fluctuates rapidly, we get cranky and lose mental clarity and ability to stay on task. Furthermore, there can be loss of muscle strength, stamina, and fine motor coordination. It is easy to see the pattern in children. Cyanide Hour occurs late in the afternoon when the kids are ready for dinner and it is not on the table. Mom may still be at the grocery store buying dinner ingredients. There can be tears, arguments, and worse. It's no wonder Mom opens a package of cookies and offers them to the screamers so everyone survives the checkout line. By the time the meal is on the table, her child's blood sugar levels are too high because of the cookie sugar entering his/her blood stream and her child is not too interested in the healthy choices found on the dinner table. Negative behavior patterns get created, and the rest can become the foundation of poor nutritional habits.

Guess what? The same thing happens in adults. Traffic accidents and road rage returning from work may be higher than those projected based on fatigue alone. When an adult does not eat a healthy breakfast or lunch, they may be compounding end-of-day fatigue. Greeting the family at the end of the commute with a grump rather than a grin sets up another negative behavior cascade.

What about high blood sugar, the precursor to diabetes? Excess insulin production is the result of years of stress combined with poor food choices. The body cells become resistant to properly utilizing insulin in order to make energy from food. The pancreas dumps even more insulin to correct the cells' resistance and insulin blood levels continue to rise. This is referred to as hyper-insulinism. The body tries to lower excess insulin by *spilling sugar* in the urine. This is a late symptom of this imbalance and a sign of diabetes.

So what works to negotiate eating what we need, rather than what we want? Here are a few methods I've tried with my patients before we allow blood sugar levels to spiral or drop off the charts. See if any work for you.

Be gentle with yourself. **Set incremental goals**. I have one patient who could commit to eating one cooked meal of protein and veggies per week to start. He gradually built on his personal record of success. By the end of the first year, he was eating two meals a day where there was adequate protein and veggies and he was feeling much better. He said he stuck to it because he made conscious choices on *his own* terms.

Planning: One teenager, his mother, and I created a list of acceptable nutritious snacks. His mother agreed to have them available at home, in lunches, and for visiting pals. He agreed to consume them.

Prioritize eating wholesome food before fast food. Eat protein, oils, fruits, and vegetables before tanking up on refined grain-source carbohydrates and refined sugars.

Build on your Success.

Do you need suggestions for easy to grab healthy snacks? I'm a fan of fresh vegetables and fruits cut in advance and stored in the refrigerator for crispness. You can include organically grown colored peppers, celery, carrots, jicama, rutabaga, daikon, radishes, and peas in the pod. Pre-cut fruit works when sprinkled with lemon juice. I also keep a variety of olives, pickled herring, smoked salmon, yogurt, kefir, cottage cheese, and liver paté in the refrigerator. I keep bee pollen, fresh fruit, unsulphured dried fruits such as pears, apples, persimmon, apples, cherries, figs, peaches, apricots, and currants as well as nuts, and natural dried beef, turkey, and salmon jerky in the cooler. When all else fails, have a supply of veggie and predigested whey protein powder or pills accessible. Most of these transport to the office or in the car easily.

Ordinary Foods, Extraordinary Results

In Chinese medical theory, a properly balanced diet of REAL food is how we are meant to keep ourselves healthy. Adequate protein and fat intake regulate brain chemistry to keep us happy, energetic, and intelligent. Vegetables and fruits supply nutrients as well as act to eliminate waste from the body. There is no one perfect diet. There are food ratios that work well for different people. Many foods both ordinary and exotic are included in an abundant array of ingredients to keep us on track. Fish, game, meat, insects, blubber, eggs, nuts, seeds, soy, poi, rice, corn, potatoes, vegetables, and fruits from countless culinary traditions have evolved over long periods of time into balanced diets and sustain populations who live in all latitudes and longitudes.

I challenge anyone, however, to defend processed, adulterated, devitalized prepared products with extensive shelf life as food. Many of the chemical extraction agents and additives used in these products do not even need to be labeled under the law. Many people are allergic to some of these agents that are legally allowed to be used and are consumed without knowledge or consent. The list of additives would take pages of newsprint to disclose.

We have become mental in our eating habits, "you need to give a specific reason why eating a certain vegetable will benefit" people, according to Dr. Kirk Parkin, food science professor at University of Wisconsin. "If you simply tell the public that eating vegetables is good for them, you don't get much of a response," he continues. Our mothers and grandmothers have always told us to "eat your vegetables". That makes eating them even easier to discount. Now Dr.

Parkin has taken the effort to research some of our basic veggies—beets, kale, corn, green beans, and garlic. He finds they contain an abundance of protective proteins, called phase 2 enzymes, that work with other proteins to detoxify and eliminate cancer-causing entities in the liver and other parts of the body.

In fact, in recently published research, Parkin demonstrated that beets increased these helpful enzyme levels by twofold; green beans by fivefold; kale by eightfold; and sweet corn by an amazing thirteen fold! Is that enough of a mental argument to encourage some of you to eat your vegetables?

Many of the herbs I use in Benedictine Healing Products are the ordinary ones that grow in my garden and all around us as well as the exotic ones that are highly advertised. Don't you wish that people understood the Extraordinary value and nature of the Ordinary? The combination of the Ordinary and the Extraordinary is powerful.

"The combination of the Ordinary and the Extraordinary is powerful."

Holiday Gift Giving

Way beyond the noise, glitter, and gluttony that can mark a holiday season, I give thanks and blessings for my family, my community, and the work I have chosen that nourishes me.

When it comes to holiday shopping, here are a few guidelines to incorporate in order to satisfy a certain portion of your gift list. First make or buy big-ticket items early, as they often need research. For example, one of my daughters painted a portrait of her sister in October, but still needs to make a frame. Give yourself the gift of TIME. Second, make some gifts at home, either herbal or culinary, or at a local garden center. As I drive around town, inspirational ideas about appealing gifts for loved ones often pop into my head. If I am smart, I write them down. Third, find gifts for loved ones in everyday surroundings. One year my 94-year-old neighbor, Ruth, gave us a bag of pine cones from her tree for our fireplace. As we threw each one into the fire, I was reminded of her thoughtfulness. When making your purchases, support local artists and businesses.

This year, I'm going to give a friend a miniature "winter garden." It will include varieties of kale, lettuce, garlic, onions, and herbs in a big pot for the deck of their apartment.

Cooking, preserving and the drying of foodstuffs is a favorite at our house—dried jerky, lemon curd, chocolate truffles, and lemon liquors are on the list this year. My daughter and I started an extravagant vanilla bean extract some time ago. We continue to look for unusual bottles in which to present it.

I like to share decorated bags filled with garden abundance such as evergreen boughs, pinecones, dried flora, and seeds for butterfly plants.

Of course, I give herbal preparations to groups of friends. Usually I decorate a basket of oils, tinctures, and pet products and allow friends to make their own selection. Watching adults become as excited as children and talk about themselves in a candid way as part of their decision-making process is especially gratifying. A bit of my spirit goes from my home to theirs.

Here are some favorite **Benedictine** herbal formulas to give as gifts: **Rose Geranium Massage Oil** (youthful skin), **Holiday Bitters** (digestion - good tasting), **Diaper Rash Oil** (for baby bottoms), **Chill Out** (who doesn't need to relax?), **Mega Ginseng** (energy booster), **Sight Saver** (maturing eyes), **Memory Tonic, California Poppy** (for sleep), **Eleutherococcus, Immunity Plus** or **Reishi** (stamina and immunity), or **Boo Boo Juice** (every family needs one for day-to-day cuts and scratches). **Pet and Kids Products** are also popular gifts. When you purchase and use any **BHP** products, a little of my spirit goes home with you as well.

"Give yourself the gift of TIME."

29

Holiday Herbs

Herbs come into focus during the holidays. Sage and thyme accompany the aroma of Thanksgiving turkey; cloves and ginger dominate pumpkin pie; cinnamon in mulled cider and apple pie; nutmeg and vanilla in eggnog; the importance of frankincense and myrrh predate their Christian significance as do the smell of pine, fir, and spruce; saffron, sandalwood, pomegranate, persimmon, tangerine, lemon, orange, and grapefruit all deepen our experience of celebration surrounding the winter solstice.

The holidays are a great time to create herbal gifts that heal and delight. I love to spend time in my garden harvesting or in the kitchen concocting, and I encourage my friends and patients to do the same. Some gifts I have made in the past include: rose moisturizer, lavender sachets and soaps, cedar oil, holiday herbal potpourri, chamomile and rosemary shampoo, tea tree hair conditioner; bergamot, jasmine, sassafras and violet tea, savory salt, licorice and lemon drops, basil pesto, and anise cookies.

In addition to herbs from the garden, I'll harvest seeds and plants for gifts. I am passionate about the California butterfly corridor and invite friends and patients to join the collective effort by ceasing the use of pesticides in their gardens and planting plants that support the butterfly lifecycle. Go to www.butterflyproject.org for more info and photos. Plant California pipevine, plantain, life everlasting, passion vine, and milkweed to encourage butterfly pupation and nectaring. Children love to receive flower and vegetable seed packets along with a promise to help them prepare the soil and plant the seeds in spring. As there is such a difference in flavor between commercial and homegrown herbal teas, mix organic fennel, chamomile flowers, and mint for a custom herbal tea blend. Freshly dried dill weed and seed, basil, and thyme smell incredibly inviting and make wonderful gifts. Adding a few rose petals, borage, or bergamot flowers to the mix is colorful as well as healthy. Dried flowers and seed pods from various trees make thoughtful arrangements. Some easy ones to start with include hydrangea flowers, watsonia seed stems, poppy heads, and cones from evergreen trees. Culinary herb wreaths are excellent gifts that are appreciated meal after meal.

From the kitchen comes the most delicious application of fresh herbs. Herb-flavored unpasteurized vinegars using basil, tarragon, raspberries, or garlic presented in unusual bottles make attractive gifts. I love to make holiday treats such as poppy seed cake with pecans. There are two special Dutch holiday cookies I grew up with—marzipan made from almonds and spicklas made with nutmeg, cinnamon, cloves, and mace. For very special people on your gift list, splurge and make vanilla bean extract or use saffron in a holiday recipe or two.

Benedictine Healing Products makes over one hundred handcrafted herbal products for infants, children, adults, and pets. If you do not have time to make your own, try some of ours.

"The holidays are a great time to create herbal gifts that heal and delight."

Spring Cleaning

In Chinese theory, spring starts on Chinese New Year. As the days lengthen and the weather warms, they advise to continue wearing warm clothes a little longer than most of us are apt to do to correct for a sudden wind or last minute chill. In our mild Santa Cruz climate, it is also a good time to consider a short cleansing program to acknowledge the shift from winter to summer metabolism.

The purpose of a cleansing is to become more invigorated. For those who live life in the fast lane, you may wish to embark on a modified program of cleansing. In order to maintain energy and protect immunity, it is important to decrease intake and increase elimination of toxic body waste material that may have accumulated over time. Here are a few tips for very busy people.

Spring cleaning happens in the mind, body and spirit levels of our being. First, decide how long a period of time you wish to dedicate for the purpose of this cleansing. One day? Three days? A week? Then, look at your calendar and clear a space where you have as few obligations as your life permits. Plan the time to get more rest. Go to bed earlier. Get up earlier if necessary to complete tasks as body cleansing occurs primarily in the evening and in the deep of night. During the time you are asleep between sunset and midnight, the brain is 3 times more active in cellular repair than it would be if you were awake during that time.

Plan age and ability matched exercise and stretching. Drink plenty of water afterwards as body movement–especially twisting–increases waste removal. Yoga, Tai Chi, or Chi

Gung are ancient and well-considered systems of regulating the breath of the body and toning every muscle, tendon, and ligament without injury, if executed with proper training. Another means of increasing blood oxygen is laughter! Read a humorous book or watch a movie that tickles your funny bone.

Food ratios and choices are important. Eating slowly, and chewing each mouthful a long time to absorb the tastes of each meal is the way the organs of digestion and assimilation prepare to secrete the proper enzymes for optimum digestion. Be certain that all the flavors–bitter, sour, pungent, salty, and sweet–are represented at each meal. Easy to digest or cooked food, in Chinese terms, lightens the work of the digestive tract as well. Enzymes are not destroyed until about 118 degrees Fahrenheit, so lightly cooked vegetables improve assimilation according to Chinese theory. For example, you may decide to use nutrient broths such as bone broth or vegetarian broths that you have prepared and frozen prior to your cleanse. Adding fresh vegetables and cooking spices rich in antioxidants and super nutrients, such as garlic, ginger, basil, oregano, thyme, parsley and sage, is tasty and quick. Protein is the building block of cellular renewal and stamina. It is very important when cleansing to consume adequate protein so the organs of elimination—the skin, lungs, kidneys, liver and digestive tract—can perform their functions more efficiently to enhance elimination of bodily waste. It is a mistake to fast and allow the digestive tract to stagger into stasis. Digestive stagnation actually increases bodily waste. Some people find using predigested whey or brown rice protein powder a very handy shortcut to accomplish this goal.

As most enzymes are readily available mid-morning and early afternoon and to a lesser extent in the early evening, I recommend protein and vegetables at breakfast and lunch and a smaller portion at dinner. Eat a great variety of vegetables daily. Put a minimum of ten (it's easier than it sounds) veggies in each nutrient broth or salad and use some different ones at the next meal. Be wise about what you use as your fuel. It's the only body you have and it should perform well your entire life!

Blood Root Plus is a great herbal formula to support your spring cleansing.

"During the time you are asleep between sunset and midnight, the brain is 3 times more active in cellular repair than it would be if you were awake during that time."

Herbal Weight Loss

The resolution to lose weight is an expression of hope for change and improvement. People often seek support to accomplish this by soliciting their practitioners, visiting diet centers, and using diet products. As dieters tackle the daunting task of limiting culinary intake, they undergo a process of awareness and discipline: an increased degree of self-actualization. To some this may sound high falutin' and irrelevant, but I believe it occurs with every breath, meal, and act of kindness. As John Lennon said, "Life is what happens while you're making other plans."

So, where to start? Losing weight isn't rocket science, although the media still attempts to make it sound incredibly scientific. It still boils down to, "exercise more and eat moderate amounts of the right things at the right time of the day." I haven't found the one perfect diet for everyone to follow, so I am saved from becoming a guru. Evidence is rapidly accumulating that food in its natural (organic, unprocessed) state allows the body to have the best chance of converting food to energy with fewer side-effects such as inflammation, self-intoxication, and fatigue. There are common sense guidelines to follow but the fine tuning needs to be done on an individual basis while considering variables such as heritage, food allergies, time constraints, cooking abilities, season of the year, and the energy requirements of the lifestyle one shoulders.

Exercise is the other half of the equation. Exercise benefits are cumulative to maintain body muscle mass over time. Choose the kinds of movement that are appealing. Stretching and gentle movement of all the joints are especially important. Raising the pulse rate to 115 beats per minute for 15 minutes daily encourages the body to construct additional blood supply to the heart. Walking may be one of the best exercises to enhance the mind, body, and spirit.

In response to a request from the fabulous Santa Cruz, CA diet queen, Cheri Bianchini, I composed an herbal formula, **Diet Aid**. It does not rely on purgatives, strong diuretics, ephedra or herbal stimulants. What's left? Herbs that support energy; decrease insulin resistance and normalize blood sugar levels; motivate thyroid; improve assimilation of food and clear stomach stagnation. It contains tyrosine, chromium picolinate, and L-carnitine which convert fat to muscle and increase basal metabolic rate. One herb even takes the edge off the user's appetite. It does not promise you can eat all you want, not exercise, and still lose weight, however **Diet Aid** is safe and effective. It works to enhance a weight loss program, increase muscle tone, energy, and metabolic rate. Everyone wants a miracle when it comes to weight loss–an effortless phenomenon that occurs while we sleep. I suggest that taking charge of your life is a miracle that happens meal by meal.

"The resolution to lose weight is an expression of hope…"

"…taking charge of your life is a miracle that happens meal by meal."

A reader asked for guidelines while using herbal support when trying to lose weight. As a practitioner, I'm not in favor of starvation or fad diets. I'd rather people establish appropriate ratios of food groups–protein, vegetables, oils, fruits, and grains–and eat plenty of fresh unprocessed organic foods. In my clinical experience, this usually means superior quality protein, excellent quality non-hydrogenated or interesterified oils, unpasteurized dairy products and a minimum of grain-source carbohydrates. However, if it is important for you to slim down, here are some safe herbs I use to assist in the process.

First one must concentrate on detoxification and tonification of the intestinal tract. I use the gentle **Butternut Bark Plus** to move food and metabolic waste through the intestinal system without causing strong gripping or upsetting the water-mineral balance in the intestine. To provide a balanced formula for the kidney and bladder and provide a slight diuretic action, I use **Kidney Care** to enhance excretion of cellular waste as well as water through the urinary system.

The next category of herbal support to consider is a formula to enhance fat metabolism by the liver. For this, **No Burp** is excellent especially if added to a cup of green or black tea. This mixture harmonizes the action of the stomach and the liver to improve digestive discomfort as well as fat metabolism. Along this same line, if a person has deposits of cellulite, which is a mix of fat and metabolic waste deposited in fat cells, using another product, **Lymph Oil,** has been very successful. Lymph Oil works by vigorous rubbing and squeezing of the cellulite areas with the oil, which stimulates circulation to the cells and encourages the release, and then elimination of the metabolic waste.

To reduce hunger drive it is important to enhance utilization of the good quality food you ingest. One of my favorite methods is to encourage the use of herbal bitters to improve assimilation of food. If you assimilate food that is consumed efficiently and the cells of the body satisfy their nutritional requirements, the brain shuts down the physical part of the hunger drive. To achieve this goal, I recommend **Holiday Bitters,** a pleasant tasting formula blending more than thirty herbs and taken before meals. If there is prolific gas and bloating, **Tummy Ease** is an excellent blend of European and Chinese herbs to address this digestive issue.

I think it is equally important to address fatigue. One of the most frequent complaints I hear from patients when dieting is they get so tired they start reaching for sugar and carbs. To avoid this, I recommend an herbal energy tonic such as **Eleutherococcus** or **Mega Ginseng,** a blend of ten different kinds of energy tonic herbs.

Finally, when dieting, nurture yourself by increasing exercise, relaxation, and sleep.

"...establish appropriate ratios of food groups— protein, vegetables, oils, fruits, and grains—and eat plenty of fresh unprocessed organic foods..."

Everyone Knows You Should Exercise

Everyone knows you should exercise, but did you know the enormous body of research substantiating the health claims for exercising? Perhaps you noticed the Harvard study published in May (2002) where men were tested for the effects of exercise and the lack of it at age twenty and again thirty years later at age fifty. Even though the fifty-year-olds were out of shape at the beginning of the study, after a protracted exercise regime, their performance approached their personal twenty-year-old output!

There are certainly many kinds of exercise. Choose something you like that is age and body-type appropriate, and matches your personal, work, and living style. For example, I find that what works for me is to do something with other people such as walking, dancing, a yoga or qigong class, tennis or gardening.

The important thing is moving your muscles and body gracefully within your muscle range and in a relaxing context, where stress can be reduced.

There is a book, *Strong Women Stay Young* by Miriam Nelson, Ph.D, that counts the advantages of two forty-minute exercise sessions for women ages 65 through 92 completed at Tufts Medical School in Boston. After six months of a series of simple stretches and exercises performed with no fancy equipment, members of the study group needed less reliance upon walkers or wheelchairs, fewer medications or reduced dosage of medications, they slept better, had better appetites, and had a profound enhancement of *joie de vivre*. This is true for men too.

This sounds too good to be true. If you were reading an advertisement making health claims of this breadth and magnitude, I'd be the first to suggest *caveat emptor*, or *let the buyer beware*. In the case of exercise, however, I throw my hat into the 'pro' exercise ring with conviction. It has taken me a number of years to get into the groove in my own life patterns. Each year I've been able to increase the amount of time dedicated in my day to body movement. Each time I dance, or go to a Yoga class, or walk or hike with friends, I honestly wonder why I have had so much resistance. I really love the way I feel during and afterwards. I extend the invitation to all readers to find out for themselves the joys of frequent exercise.

For those of you who need a little more convincing, I have collated the bottom line from a number of various medical studies and summarized the beneficial effects of exercise for you below. Each of the benefits listed in the next paragraph is a conclusion from an actual research project. There is a good reason listed for everyone. I invite you to begin including exercise for fun and health into your plans this year.

Here are twenty-five reasons to exercise:

Exercise improves immunity, strengthens bones, prevents cancer, improves stress tolerance, prevents insomnia, prevents constipation, prevents anxiety, prevents depression, increases activity of anti-aging enzymes, increases endorphins, slows neuromuscular aging, reduces body fat, simplifies weight control, improves insulin response, reduces blood pressure, increases reaction time, improves the body's ability to dissolve blood clots, increases physical work capacity, increases maximum oxygen intake, enlarges coronary arteries for better blood circulation, improves the heart's pumping action, increases cardiac output, reduces resting heart rate, gives glowing light through the skin, and improves sex life.

"...members of the study group needed less reliance upon walkers or wheelchairs, fewer medications or reduced dosage of medications, they slept better, had better appetites, and had a profound enhancement of *joie de vivre*."

Salad Dressing is Good for your Skin

Jody, a nine-year-old with eczema was brought to the clinic for a traditional Chinese medical analysis and treatment. After doing an evaluation and *tuina*, a gentle stimulation of points on the skin for children, I recommended the parents massage the child with **Rose Geranium Massage Oil** twice a day.

Dietary recommendations included serving the child a soft egg yolk and fish once a day, vegetables, good quality oils, grain-source carbohydrates three times a day, and fresh fruit twice a day along with plenty of water. The oils should be extra-virgin expeller pressed, or unrefined and not contain any traces of extracting agents. The eggs should be free of any cracks, antibiotics, or hormones; and come from cage-free birds fed organic food that can scratch the earth and keep themselves healthy. She was to avoid refined sugar; fruit juice; and refined, hydrogenated and partially hydrogenated oils; especially corn, sunflower, cottonseed, soy, and canola.

I treated the child twice a month for two months and once a month four additional months before the skin was completely clear.

The parents couldn't figure how to include fish daily without turning THEIR lives upside down. I suggested a modified Caesar salad dressing that was appealing to Jody to be used on days the family did not serve another fish. Over the years I've used this suggestion successfully with parents and children alike.

Here is the recipe:

1-4 anchovy filets per serving (or anchovy paste)

¼ to ½ lemon juiced

1-2 tsp unpasteurized vinegar (balsamic, apple cider, or wine)

1 Tbsp extra-virgin olive oil

½ to 1 tsp flaxseed oil or ¼ to ½ tsp Nordic Naturals orange-flavored Arctic cod liver oil

Fresh squeezed garlic (1 clove)

Large flake black pepper (to taste)

Sea salt (to taste)

Freshly ground imported aged Reggiano Parmesan cheese

Salad ingredients vary depending on the season and what you find in the refrigerator or garden. Try to include at least ten different vegetables. I'll use a mixture of spring salad greens and large leaf lettuces, avocado, tomato, colored peppers, varieties of onion, cucumber, jicama, apple, pear, orange, grated carrots, cabbage, daikon, and beets. Sometimes I'll steam broccoli, cauliflower, rutabaga, or turnips and add them on top of the fresh ingredients before tossing the salad. Add raw or toasted nuts. Rotate and increase the variety of these vegetables.

Dress and toss the salad. Sprinkle cheese on top or add a dab of sheep feta or fresh goat cheese on the side. It's a meal in itself.

The herbal massage oil should contain a variety of soothing and anti-microbial properties and no preservatives. When selecting an oil look for it to contain shea butter, extra-virgin olive, jojoba, coconut, or almond oils, with vitamin A and E to prevent them from becoming rancid. The healing herbs might include rose geranium, St. John's Wort, and chamomile, as they are soothing. Calendula, mugwort, thyme, yarrow, and celandine provide more direct support for the skin. Glycerin should be avoided in topical preparations as it is drying to the deep layer of skin cells and perpetuates the cycle of skin dryness.

The protein and omega 3 fatty acids found in fish, flaxseed, and soft egg yolks are very helpful in nourishing the skin, hair, joints and nervous system. The herbal massage oil is a powerful topical source of nutrient that can be partially absorbed through the skin. I prefer an oil rather than a salve as the oil can be drizzled over the body without having to be rubbed into painful skin sores. Some sores are so deep and infected that you may wish to wrap the area with plastic wrap after applying the herb oil to keep the sore moist with oil overnight. Sometimes applying aloe vera gel to cool the inflammation of eczema is also useful. Oatmeal baths can also offer relief until the internal nutrients begin to repair the skin cells. However, in Jody's case, it was the salad dressing that made the difference.

.

Chocolate

Whoever heard of a health practitioner promoting chocolate for your **health?**

Over thirty years ago when a friend gave me a barrel of roasted cocoa beans, I thought how much I liked to eat chocolate: dark rich chocolate. It also started recollections about chocolate. There were the nickel ice cream cones we bought at the drug store and consumed listening to the outdoor band concerts on warm summer Friday nights. Dad ordered strawberry, Mom and I ordered chocolate. Chocolate came at holiday times. Loft's or Fanny Farmer's chocolate came in the shape of Santa Claus at Christmas, hearts at Valentine's Day, and bunnies or fudge and walnut filled eggs at Easter. Uncle George told of sharing the Hershey bars from Aunt Millie's World War II care packages with eager French children. Hot cocoa sparked enthusiasm on cold winter mornings, noons, and nights. Chocolate. Chocolate. Chocolate. As I grew older chocolate was supposed to be avoided by any teenager who wanted clear skin. That meant every time I ate it and did not suffer acne "flowers," I got away with something. People I knew growing up treated eating chocolate like sharing a secret or falling off the wagon. This gave the subject additional caché.

As an herbalist and champion of the plant kingdom, however, I began collecting information about the brown beans. Could something so universally loved also be healthy for people? Here's a short encapsulation of my findings.

History of Chocolate

Columbus discovered chocolate on the island of Guanaja near Honduras during his fourth voyage and made note of it, although little became of the encounter. Cortez was the first European on record to bring the beans to Spain. It became fashionable throughout Europe after 1615 when Anne, a Spanish princess, married Louis XIII of France and brought her affection for chocolate with her to the French court. From there, it spread throughout Europe.

Chocolate beans come from the cacao tree. Archeological indication exists that cacao has grown in the Amazon and Orinoco River complexes for the last six thousand years. From this origin the tree was brought both north and south to the different empires of the Aztec, Toltec, and Mayan populations. Aztec lore relates that the god, Quetzalcoatl', founder of the race, designated cacao as a divine gift and used it both to stem fatigue and provide pleasure. Cacao beans were used as units of exchange. There exist legends about the proliferation of cacao trees. The Aztecs believed that a drink of "xocolatl", meaning bitter water, stimulated mental and psychic awareness. Gradually, by default rather than intent, cacao began being used as a beverage by the Spanish. They noticed it increased stamina and strength and did "not lead to drunkenness." But it was bitter. Then some nameless person began to Europeanize the substance by adding sugar, cinnamon, vanilla, aniseed, and pepper. Finally, someone served it hot—hot chocolate! Over the next two hundred years different European countries made their peace with chocolate and integrated it into their cuisine and culture. It became so popular, there were chocolate houses similar to Starbucks all over Europe. The first British factory opened in 1728.

It was the Swedish botanist, Linnaeus, however, who gave the Latin name "Theobroma" to this beloved substance. "Theo" means god and "broma" means food. Food of the Gods!

Historical Uses of Chocolate

Historically, chocolate has been used for the weak and infirm; as having curative powers: a panacea; curing consumption; consolation for lovers' misfortunes; upset stomach; hangovers; mild fevers; senility; phlegmatic temperament; gout; to relieve fatigue; as a diuretic and antiseptic; for cough, snake bite, burns, wounds; for dry eyes, alopecia; as an emmenagogue, for pregnancy and parturition; for high blood pressure; as a brain stimulant; as an antispasmodic; as a dentifrice. Any of these sound familiar?

Chocolate Composition

What is in the composition of chocolate that makes it so unique and useful? Carbohydrates, fat (as cocoa butter that is easily assimilated), ash, protein, and water comprise chocolate, a nutrient dense food that makes available a high amount of energy per unit weight. It has been included in astronauts' and sports players' diets. Depending upon its form, it contains 400 to 800 calories for 100g (3½ oz). It is abundant in minerals: magnesium, potassium, calcium, sodium, zinc, iron, and copper. Add vitamins A, B1, B2, C, D, E. It contains theobromine, a molecule related to caffeine, as well as one-fifth the amount of caffeine in an equivalent amount of coffee. Polyphenols or flavonoids are antioxidants in chocolate. This is why it doesn't go rancid. It also contains tyramine and phenylethylamine (PEA). PEA is called the "love drug". Research exists that allies PEA and its metabolites with other substances that elevate moods. Several fatty acids act on the cannabinoid and opioid receptors and neurotransmitters in the brain that some researchers associate with feeling good.

My Observations

In my acupuncture practice I give roasted cacao beans to women who are experiencing PMS or are menopausal. I find it very useful for depression associated with hormone fluctuations. Although this clinical observation is not supported by research, my patients report relief. I do not eliminate it for teenagers who come for adolescent skin concerns. I encourage competitive sports participants to use it as part of their training. Finally, when people are older or have a wasting disease, have a poor appetite, or need to maintain or increase weight, cacao is invaluable added to a whey protein powder.

However, there is an obvious difference between what I am recommending and Hershey Kisses. I do not recommend milk chocolate or mixing refined sugar with chocolate. Unfortunately this is the form most accessible commercially. Instead, when making cocoa use raw steamed milk, or unsweetened almond or soy milk and mix in unsweetened cocoa. Purchase or make your own chocolate delights without adding refined sugar. Use maple syrup, maple sugar, date sugar, raw cane sugar, stevia, fructose, dried fruit or sweet fruits such as persimmons. It's easy to do and delicious. Very dark chocolate is available. My daughter found 99% chocolate bars on the Internet for me for the holidays last year. 70% to 85% chocolate bars are becoming more available. Happily, as more consumers request unsweetened cocoa and chocolate at their favorite restaurants and stores, the more available it will become.

Chinese Theory

In Chinese medicine, it is important to train the palate especially of children to include and appreciate all the flavors - sour, sweet, pungent, salty, and bitter. Hot cocoa is a wonderful and easy beverage for a parent to use to accomplish bitter. It's amazing how the palate is capable of becoming educated.

Recipes

There are a multitude of cookbooks with fabulous chocolate recipes. Read them for inspiration and modify them to omit refined sugar. Some recipes will work better than others. Here are a few that have worked for me.

Hot cocoa can be made with heated or steamed raw milk and pure cocoa powder. Try it with a little honey cinnamon, nutmeg and chili powder. I use Fair Trade organic brands.

Fresh and dried fruit dipped in chocolate with the above-listed sweeteners can be served quickly. My favorites include strawberries, pineapple, cherries, raspberries, apricots, dates, currants, prunes, and persimmon wedges. They are so sweet in themselves, the chocolate needs next to no sweetener.

Stuffing nuts - brazil, pecan, walnuts, almonds - in the dried fruit multiplies the possibilities. I make a cookie and a brownie with nut flour, a variety of sweeteners, and pure chocolate nips mixed with semi-sweet chocolate morsels.

There are very dark chocolate bars including Newman's Own Organics and Richard Donnellly's 70% bar and Michel Cluizel's 99% bar. Add shaved bitter chocolate on top of other dishes containing meat and veggies inspired by the molé of Mexican cuisine.

Finally, I adore organic coconut, fresh or dried, with chocolate, nuts, and dried fruit.

Now you've heard of a health practitioner promoting chocolate.

"Could something so universally loved also be healthy for people?"

Herbs for Pregnancy and Nursing

In January 2004 Santa Cruz was honored by a visit of one of America's premier midwives, Ina May Gaskin, who popularized home birth with her book *Spiritual Midwifery*. She spoke fervently and openly about the experiences of birthing 2028 women and their babies on The Farm in Tennessee, a retreat she founded with her husband, Steven Gaskin. She spoke of some of the procedures that worked for them and observations made that kept childbirth safe and sacred for those 2028 women. In fact, there was not a single maternal mortality and an extremely low rate (less than 7%) of any complication on The Farm.

Statistics on hospital births routinely omit many major pregnancy complications from their statistics. Non-vaginal delivery and birth on demand are becoming more acceptable. C-section rates vary by doctor and hospital from 20-80%. Mainstream obstetrical practitioners would do well to read her books to learn from her experience.

Apart from a woman's choice of working with a medical doctor or midwife, or both, there are herbs that are helpful for expectant mothers. Teas or tinctures are a lovely form for ease of ingestion—slowly, warm, relaxing.

Pre-pregnancy, include nettles, mint, and red clover blossoms. During pregnancy include fennel, nettles, and red raspberry in your tea. For morning sickness, increase your blood sugar level with tea and toast with honey **before** rising. Increase protein in the diet as well. Tea may include peach leaves, peppermint, ginger, and wild yam. For varicose veins prevention, use oatstraw, nettles, and parsley. A compress of witch hazel, comfrey, mullein, yarrow, and oak bark is useful.

If anemia is a concern, include nettles, yellow dock and dandelion root. As pregnancy proceeds, if heartburn is an uncomfortable experience, consider fennel, anise, lemon, lime and papaya. If the bladder is irritated, a tea of yarrow and urva ursi is helpful. While high blood pressure is a serious symptom, a tea of nettles, red raspberry, parsley, passion flower, hawthorn, and skullcap is soothing. If there is concern of pre-eclampsia, in addition to protein, potassium and calcium, a tea of nettles, dandelion and red raspberry are useful nutritional additions. Finally for a peaceful centered feeling, tea of motherwort, blessed thistle, red raspberry, spearmint, burdock, and sarsaparilla is lovely.

Pregnancy is a very personal decision that some segments of our culture try to politicize and others to market. I wish to go on record as one woman who feels fortunate to have had three wonderful home births. When I did my personal research to find either a birth coach, doctor, practitioner, and/or midwife, as my first consideration, I looked for safety for the baby and me. The statistics worldwide support those of Ina Mae's: at least in an uncomplicated pregnancy, home is the safest place for a baby to be born 97% of the time.

"...home is the safest place for a baby to be born..."

Graceful Menopause

Fifty years of the artificial women's hormone replacement industry crashed with the publication of the National Women's Health Network book, <u>The Truth About Hormone Replacement Therapy</u>. It was reviewed on the front page of the *New York Times*. Doctors urged their patients to cease hormone replacement (HRT). Tens of thousands of women were thrown into a frenzy. One patient's response was, "I've been taking Premarin for 25 years. Now they tell me it may cause cancer? What do I do now for the unpleasant symptoms for which it had been first prescribed?"

I've been a partner through menopause to thousands of women. The most astonishing observation is, no two women have traveled this passage in the same way. The tools I use-- herbs, nutraceuticals, homeopathy, and acupuncture—are the same or similar, but the specific selection, dosage, timing, and combination are different, just as women are different.

Here are some of my observations as well as basic guiding principles and keys to mitigating menopausal symptoms. First, menopause is a normal life passage. Like other changes in the life cycle, it is not supposed to be too burdensome. If there are extremes, it is helpful to play Sherlock and uncover some root sources of distress. Review your lifestyle critically and decide on the appropriate changes in water intake, sleep, exercise, and nutrition that may be necessary to accommodate this metamorphosis in your life. There is broad latitude in selection of personal dietary choices as long as there are adequate amounts of excellent quality oils, protein, vegetables, and fruits. There is a more narrow definition of what constitutes nutritious food, however: the best being non-

GMO, less hybridization, low or no processing, grass-fed and organic. Eat a great variety of warmed foods on time.

Check out your emotional diet as well. Not satisfied with yourself or the situation? Menopause is a green light to make positive changes. Get the support you need. Learn to assess the value of your commitments.

Exercise is critical to a sense of well being in the second half of life. Stretching is the key to flexibility and function. Select your movement choices carefully.

For herbal support to balance hormones first consider **Menopause Plus**, a formula containing **vitex** or **chasteberry** along with other herbs and homeopathic remedies. If specific issues feel daunting, isolate them and make informed choices of other herbs to include. **Menopause Plus** is a starting point that is by no means exhaustive. Try **Motherwort** for anxiety; **California Poppy** for insomnia; **Feverfew** for headache; **Hormonal Acne Relief** (Blue Vervain) for hormonal acne; **Horsetail** for urinary incontinence; **Passion Flower** to relax and regain your sense of humor; **Horse Chestnut** for varicose veins; **Memory Tonic** for forgetfulness; **Xiao Yao Plus** for breast tenderness or feeling blue; **Eleutherococcus, Herbal Mineral Tonic** and **Nettles** for fatigue; **Lymph Oil** to massage cellulite; **Yoni Oil** for vaginal dryness and low libido; and **Blessed Thistle** or **Black Cohosh** for hot flashes.

You can make a graceful transition to the other side of menopause, the time of life the Chinese call Second Spring.

"Menopause is a normal life passage."

Men's Health

Men's health isn't given much press. When men do come to discuss health concerns, they overflow with symptoms, questions, and ailments, all the while feeling culturally constrained to talk about them to boot.

In Chinese theory, men's health deals directly with the heart, the source of all Yang (male) energy in the body. Despite popular belief to the contrary, laughter (the sound of the heart), tears (the liquid of the heart), exercise and hugs are important to moisten an otherwise emotional male desert. A healthy heart is an expression of a balanced male life.

A lot of the problems that come with heart imbalances—hypertension, arteriosclerosis, stress and ulcers—are prevalent in the male population. The prevention of these includes a healthy life style: adequate sleep, exercise, sex and a healthy diet with good quality organic foods whenever possible. Refrain from smoking, drink plenty of good water and consume less coffee and alcohol. Herbs such as **hawthorn berry**, **gingko**, **yarrow**, **garlic**, **ginger**, and **cayenne** are useful, as are **L. acidophilus** and **cod liver oil**.

The prostate is the first uniquely male concern. In traditional Chinese Medicine, it is considered the male second heart; the repository of male worries. Some men experience BHP - benign prostate hypertrophy (enlargement) or prostatitis (inflammation of the prostate). Studies indicate increased relaxation time (getting out of flight or fight mode), increasing water intake, eating a variety of high quality oils (seeds, nuts, and fish oils), cooking with parsley, and using vitamins E and C, and zinc are useful for prostate health.

The testicles are another uniquely male concern. Men should learn to do periodic self-exams and tell their practitioner if any changes are noted.

The penis is the final concern unique to men. Attitudes about circumcision are being discussed more openly. I personally feel it is a man's right to choose. I have yet to have a male patient of mine express regret about looking different from Dad or the other circumcised guys in the locker room because they had a foreskin. In fact, some men are disfigured by circumcision surgery. If a male child is not circumcised, it is important for parents to avoid premature retraction of the foreskin to prevent inflammation or scarring.

Safe sex is important in the discussion of penis care. It is important to be informed about condoms and spermicides and use them appropriately to prevent pregnancy and spread of STD's (sexually transmitted diseases) such as genital warts, herpes, HIV or AIDS.

Impotence is the absence of arousal. Studies indicate that few examples of impotence are physically based. Arousal issues may be a neon sign inviting deeper examination of the emotional big picture. The first male responsibility is self arousal due to creative caring thought and activity.

"In Chinese theory men's health deals directly with the heart, the source of all Yang (male) energy."

Aging Gracefully

My senior patients like to have guidelines for making an herbal cocktail to drink once or twice a day as part of their stay-healthy routine. Keeping herbs in tincture form makes this simple. People can mix and match ingredients according to individual needs as the seasons and their symptoms change. Herbs taken this way in small doses become part of a person's individual nutritional profile. When there is an aggravation of symptoms, the dose of many of these same nutritional herbs can be increased for a medicinal effect. After the episode diminishes, the dose can be decreased once again to the nutritional level.

Here are some herbal suggestions I make for different issues regarding aging.

I always start with digestion as the cornerstone of health. Seniors need to be encouraged to prepare fresh veggies, consistently consume small amounts of protein, use excellent quality oils, and enjoy adequate fresh fruit to keep the digestive tract functioning with daily regularity. Limit sugar and grain-source carbohydrates to between one and three per day. Helpful digestive herbal formulas include **Holiday Bitters** to help the stomach destroy pathogenic organisms and enhance digestion of food; **Tummy Ease** to assist in assimilation of food especially if there is gas and bloating; and **No Burp** to enhance breakdown of fats and correct burping. **Cat's Claw** is useful if there is an irritated intestinal lining. **Butternut Bark** softens the stool.

Second, in Chinese medical philosophy, rejuvenation of the blood stream helps reduce many aches and pains. Small amounts of **Blood Root Plus, Gotu Kola,** and **Horse Chestnut Tonic,** formulas that address circulation of the veins may be useful for varicose veins or hemorrhoids. Herbs that address cardiovascular circulation, such as **Dan Shen**, **Heart Health Hi,** and **Heart Health Glo** form another foundation stone of self-care.

Third, losing one's wits is a major concern of the elderly population. While minor forgetfulness is acceptable, the specter of dementia is scary and dangerous. I use **Ginkgo,** or **Memory Tonic,** a formula that contains 13 herbs known to address this issue. Additionally, 5-hydroxy-folate and Nordic Naturals' Arctic Cold Cod Liver are important to enhance memory functions.

Fourth, having enough energy to enjoy life is a major complaint of my elderly patients. Using **Siberian Ginseng**, **Ashwagandha, Astragalus, Nettles** or **Mega Ginseng**, a formula that contains ten different chi tonic herbs, will help boost energy. Each of these energy tonics has a slightly different application as individual needs vary.

Finally, conservation of vision is important in maintaining quality of life for the elderly. **Bilberry,** or **Sight Saver**, a formula containing 23 herbs that supports circulation and nutrition for the cornea and macula, has been useful for countless seniors.

These are a few of the many specific issues facing seniors where herbs can be of great assistance in providing nutritional contributions and solutions.

"Start with digestion as the cornerstone of health".

Saffron: the Anti-Aging Herb

I'm just wild about Saffron. No, not the woman referred to in the 1960's Donovan song—I'm wild about **cooking** with saffron. Saffron has been used in recipes from appetizers to desserts, in cuisines around the world. There are the deep hues of red, orange, and yellow that enhance the pleasure of foods. The incredible aroma and sophisticated taste are unsurpassed. But saffron is underutilized in American kitchens. It is time to understand its benefits.

As an herbalist I know saffron has to be the finest **anti-aging** herb ever designed. It contains lycopene, found to stabilize vision problems associated with aging—cataracts and macular degeneration. In Chinese medicine, it invigorates the blood which means it prevents strokes and heart attacks. It tastes better than aspirin and won't upset your stomach. It also disperses liver chi stagnation. This is code for taking the elephant off your chest and putting you in a better mood. Saffron has been part of medical records in India, Greece, Egypt, Persia, and Rome. Abruzzi wrote, "Saffron arouses joy in every breast, settles the stomach, gives the liver rest." In modern research saffron has been found to contain vitamin A, B1, B2, an array of antioxidants, and chemotherapeutic agents. The most recent researchers at Rutgers University are currently identifying the active compounds in saffron and trying to ascertain their mode of action on cancer cells.

Historically, saffron has been used for afflictions of everything from cardiovascular problems to black plague, improving appetite and digestion of fats, relieving rheumatoid arthritis, and inhibiting *helicobacter pylori* infections involved in stomach ulcers.

There are easy ways to include saffron in your daily diet. I use a saffron infusion in vegetable, fish (bouillabaisse), egg drop, and even miso soup. The aroma, a musky rich complexity, occurs immediately and becomes more complex over time. Add saffron in an herb mixture to a favorite recipe of seafood, chicken, lamb, eggs, paella, rice, beans, chutneys, nut and spice mixtures. A few filaments can be added to scrambled eggs along with smoked salmon and/or vegetables. Adding saffron to your favorite quiche is colorful. Using saffron in a marinade for fish, chicken or lamb for a curry or BBQ will elicit animated commentary from your consumers. Rice dishes are a perfect foil for saffron. When splurging, it can be baked in bread and desserts such as nut cakes, rice pudding as well as added to berries or ice cream.

The Rutgers researchers were explicit: saffron works better when taken by oral ingestion. What are we waiting for?

Benedictine Healing Products carries **Saffron** as we consider it a fabulous way to take charge of your health in a tantalizing and delicious way.

"...saffron has to be the finest anti-aging herb ever designed."

For your Pet, Before the Vet

Everybody loves their pets. Pets play many different roles in family structures. They are used therapeutically for the elderly, and to draw out children with special needs. In these times when families may live long distances from each other, pets may fill a void in our emotional lives. Also, as we are becoming an increasingly urban society removed from our food supply, pets are often our only connection with the animal world. I believe it is important to use high quality nutrition, adequate exercise, and emphasize the importance of preventative care in order to enhance the quality of our pets' lives. In the process, we enrich the quality of our own lives as well.

As pets become relatively more important to us, our concern for their comfort and health is also increasing. **Benedictine Healing Products** makes wonderful herbal products called **LoveMyPet** that you can use easily to assist your pet with some symptoms of discomfort and perhaps prevent them from becoming major calamities.

The feedback on these products exceeds all our expectations. It is a great relief to a pet owner to be able to make his pet more comfortable in such a caring non-toxic manner. If you try a product and the symptoms are not relieved after a week or two, please take your pet to your veterinarian.

Does your pet have any of these needs?

Stress Relief provides a calming effect especially for the pet that is not a good traveler, or upsets easily in unfamiliar or stressful conditions such as thunder, new guests, or fireworks. Caretakers can give it to pets when owners are on vacation. Groomers use it to relax pets before grooming activities.

Tummy Ease is used for relief of gas and abdominal discomfort, food allergies, occasional regurgitation, or even mild constipation. Often it takes time to figure out the best kind of food for your pet when digestive irregularities occur.

Diarrhea Relief is self-evident. One of my patients used it on several of her seven cats when she drove with them while moving across the country. Use it for occasional diarrhea. Feedback from consumers indicates that it works fast and well. Do not use it too often as it might stimulate the opposite response in your pet. Do not exceed 1 to 3 doses in a day.

Skin Comfort helps for relief of skin irritations, itching, scratching, excess licking, hot spots, eczema and allergic skin reactions. Animals that are under-exercised may have skin problems. There are some animal breeds that characteristically have skin problems.

Kidney Bladder Relief is useful for pets with urinary inability, frequency, or mild inflammation or infection.

Stinky Ear Oil is a safe topical application for pets plagued by fungal ear infections or viral skin infections that give rise to unpleasant odor or constant scratching.

Joint Relief and **Immune Booster** are two formulas that address some needs of the aging pet. The **Joint Relief** is for joint pain, stiffness, and swelling associated with arthritis. Its impact is enhanced when given in tandem with Nordic Naturals fish oils.

Daily Minerals is a wonderful supplement that should precede the use of vitamins. It is 100% plant sourced and will not form stones. Give it as food daily.

Constipation Relief is self-evident for occasional constipation. If constipation is habitual, check your pet's food source and see your vet.

Immune Booster is an anti-aging support of the immune system that enhances energy, helps ward off infection, and is an amazing enhancement for many older pets.

LoveMyPet pet products are a blend of herbs and homeopathic remedies extracted in organic alcohol, water and glycerin and are easy to administer in food and water or on treats. Often your pet will lick the fluid off your hand. Putting a couple of drops on a cat's paw will cause a tidy cat to lick it off.

"It is a great relief to a pet owner to be able to make his pet more comfortable…"

Herbs and GMOs

My concern with the use of GMOs (genetically modified organisms) is that no one knows what the long-term impact on us or the environment will be. As an herbalist, I am committed to plants whose effects have been noted by keen observers for millennia. How long an evaluation period is necessary before we can reasonably conclude safety? One growing season? Twenty growing seasons? Remember thalidomide? That impacted babies of one generation, skipped a generation in others and manifested as teratogenic limbs in grandchildren of the original mothers, although their parents were born with normal limbs. By the way, thalidomide is back on the market again.

Who will set the evaluation standards for **GMOs**? Biotech firms? The government regulators who take cues from industry leaders? Can we really expect an industry to regulate itself? Remember hormone replacement therapy (HRT)? It took the Women's Health Network years to sort out the industry-generated studies from independently funded research on HRT. The conclusions of the pharmaceutical industry and those of independently funded researchers were polar opposite ("New York Times", Spring 2002).

Of course you might argue that herbs are not in the top ten crops upon which biotech firms will focus. Who is to say that interfering with the genes of one species will not affect the genes or food source of many others? We really know so little about that web. Who pollinates whom and under what circumstances? Think of the inadvertent disaster of Roundup-ready corn in our heartland on the breeding of monarch butterflies in Mexico.

Then there's the question of who will purchase our **GMO** products? One very large potato grower in the Pacific Northwest will not consider growing **GMO** potatoes as his international customers will not buy them. Most of the world has resisted U.S. government pressure to buy our **GMOs**.

What concerns do they have that we don't?

There is also a question of boundaries and fairness. Birds and the wind don't know about property lines. Many farmers stand to lose organic certification for their land because of wind and bird-spreading of **GMO** seed. Whose rights prevail when an organic farmer's crops become **GMO** contaminated by the farmer next door who has planted the "new fangled" promise from biotech?

I propose that consumers and regulators become informed and conduct a dialogue. I understand the local strawberry, rose, and carnation growers in our country are already using gene markers to identify their products for protection from theft. In our discussion we need to bring an open heart and mind as well as facts to a reality that is affecting us all.

My first recommendation is that products containing **GMOs** be labeled to allow the public to weigh in on the dialogue in this country with their dollar power as they are able to do in other countries. This is not popular with lawmakers who have campaign favors to pay, nor is it popular with supermarkets who have to risk consumer boycotts of products labeled as containing **GMOs**. The supermarkets would in turn have to pressure their suppliers to eliminate **GMOs** from products.

My second recommendation is a moratorium on the use of **GMOs** until an inclusive approach can be crafted after there is hard science. Who knows? Maybe **GMOs** are safe and can be used with impunity. I'm open to that possibility. Finally, I recommend a film about **GMOs** by Deborah Garcia, "**The Future of Food**". The future of our food chain may depend upon it. Check it out!

"GMOs ... No one knows the long-term impact..."

Your Choice: Conventional or Organic Food

There is a difference between food brought to us by conventional and organic farmers. Over the last 60 years, food production and distribution has changed from small local farmers to large syndicated agri-businesses and corporations where farm management decisions are made from Wall Street. Profits for the corporation are maximized while the fate of the farm family, nutrient content of the crop, health of the soil, quality of the water, and net effect on the environment are not considered important. The difference between these two methods of food production and distribution is alarming.

Growing up, my Dad told a story that illustrates the difference between organic and conventional farming as well as the importance of eating healthy food:

There was a farmer who had a cow. He fed the cow good grain and the cow gave plenty of good milk in return. Then the farmer got to thinking he could save some money if he began substituting a handful of sawdust for a handful of grain. He began the substitution and didn't notice any difference in the milk. So he substituted two hands full of sawdust for two hands full of grain. Again there was no difference in the milk. Thus he continued slowly substituting sawdust for grain. The farmer was happy. He was saving money. However, soon after he got that cow trained on 100% sawdust, she up and died.

I contend that much of agribusiness food is like the farmer's sawdust–devitalized at best, harmful for its additives, mishandling, and providing a false security that wholesome nutrition has been purchased.

It does cost more to provide organic food - about 30% more up front. I urge readers to bite the bullet and make the transition to organic. Why? First you'll notice food tastes better. (Just try a nice organic chicken and tell me you prefer conventionally raised chicken—or tomatoes or strawberries). Watch how much better you feel. In the long run your 30% investment in food pays off even in your paycheck with fewer sick days. All things being equal, productivity increases. As a side benefit your medical costs decrease and more importantly, you feel better.

A carefully guarded secret is learning how to read food codes to identify food sources. Conventionally farmed produce has a four-digit code. Genetically engineered foods (GMOs) have a five-digit code beginning with the number 8. Organically raised foods have a five-digit code beginning with the number 9.

In the choice between conventional and organic food, the power is in the hands of the consumer. Make a wise choice.

"Conventionally farmed produce has a four digit code. Genetically engineered foods (GMOs) have a five digit code beginning with the number 8. Organically raised foods have a five digit code beginning with the number 9."

Herbal Consumer Choice

To make an informed choice and keep open access to herbs, the consumer needs to understand there are two distinct approaches to herbal use. Although herbs have not changed over time, there are two different philosophical camps on their use and safety leading to different conclusions. The dominant philosophy changes over time, but the pattern seems to repeat. Can we learn anything about this pattern from history? In her book *Green Pharmacy*, Barbara Griggs outlines beautifully the history of herbal use. She writes how the *Regulars* (scientists) and *Irregulars* (herbalists) clashed over the use of herbs in medical practice in the 19th century. This clash is being revisited as I write.

Herbalists (*Irregulars)* who are steeped in historical use of whole herbs have observations on their safety and efficacy. They come from a point of view of working with nature and plant wisdom to modify and bring into balance a person's health issues. Although all health issues cannot be resolved simply by drinking a cup of herb tea, it often helps, and little documented harm has come to the consumer. Herbalists believe that there are a few *active* (toxic) chemicals in plants that address disease and many *buffer* chemicals that protect the consumer from the side effects of the active ingredients. In most cases there is no scientific understanding about the *buffer* components. There is also no economic incentive to look for them since herbs, *per se*, cannot be patented and large profits cannot be made on them.

Scientists (*regulars*) look at herbs, identify their most active (toxic) ingredients, and concentrate the toxic fraction to make them more potent. Plant actions such as colchicum, opium, ephedrine and valium fall into this category. In the process, they lose the buffer that protects the consumer. Then they want to restrict their use for consumer protection. For the scientist the only truth about an herb exists in terms of what the active ingredient can do. Once an herb is approved for use based on its *active ingredient*, it is usually limited to that use. One has only to look to Europe and the German Commission E document to note that based on active ingredients, herbs are officially indicated for specific restricted prescriptions.

There is room for both camps to learn much from the other. There is much for the public to gain if the information about herbs stays in public domain and access is not restricted. Both points of view have merit and can be examined with mutual respect but it takes an informed public to reason this out.

Instead, the public tends to relinquish power about healthcare to their chosen health professional. If you choose to work with an herbalist you will be told that herbs are safe and effective. If you work with a person who bases their opinion of herbs on scientific information of active ingredients, you will be told that herbs are dangerous and not to use many of them.

One hundred fifty years ago, the more powerful group, the *Regulars,* who inspired fear of herbal use, won the day and wrote history. Will the public allow this to happen again?

"...there are both *active* (toxic) chemicals in plants that address disease and *buffer* chemicals that protect the consumer from the side effects of the active ingredients."

70

Using Herbs to Change Corporate America

I just watched the movie **The Corporation,** and I started thinking about how the role of herbal use and seemingly small personal lifestyle decisions fit into the picture of evolving into a responsible global citizen. For me, there is a resonance with becoming even more dedicated to sustainable living and fostering the web of life. Having grown up on a family farm in the 40's, 50's, and 60's, I am aware of a few of the many small choices each of us can make that add up to a very BIG change in the quality of our planet. Growing herbs is one way I stay connected to the web of life.

I'm not a zealot or a purist. I drive a second-hand Swedish car, and I purchase clothes most likely made in sweatshops. Neither do I believe chamomile in my upraised fist will convert corporate America.

However, more and more of the time I opt to buy locally grown organic produce through a CSA (community sponsored agriculture) box, farmers' markets, and health food and herb stores. Most of my shopping dollar is spent at small locally owned businesses like Lloyd's Tires, Andy's Automotive, Seven Bridges Coop, Bookshop Santa Cruz, Logos, assorted tea shops and bakeries and locally owned movie theaters and restaurants. I spend advertising dollars for Benedictine Healing Products to support local organizations near and dear to my heart: music, educational and cultural events, as well as our local radio station.

Furthermore, I recycle almost everything as does much of Santa Cruz, cook from scratch, use canvas shopping bags and recycle others, shop at yard sales and second hand stores for a lot of things from clothing to gardening tools.

Finally, I teach taking personal responsibility in healthcare via my acupuncture practice by encouraging people to grow and use herbs in their daily lives. It pleases me when people share their own experiences in starting their own herb gardens. My garden is dedicated to producing more oxygen than my family consumes, re-introducing a native butterfly to the county, and producing many of the herbs used in Benedictine Healing Products formulas.

This has been a gradual process for me, as it has been brought to my attention just how much the corporate structure is diminishing the quality of our planet and my life to boot. The way I figure it, if each of us decided to do one little thing as often as possible and get a friend to do likewise, the impact over time would be amazing. We cannot turn back the clock, but we can work to change the minds of elected officials and to change laws that have allowed corporations to become so powerful, irresponsible and unaccountable.

While I chose to focus on having free access to herbs, you might contribute by focusing on some aspect of sustainable living that suits your interests. Have fun and watch the impact of your decision.

"...we can work to change the minds of elected officials and to change laws that have allowed corporations to become so powerful, irresponsible and unaccountable."

Herbs and Political Activism

Herbs have long been associated with political activism. I advocate their personal cultivation and use them as an expression of individual responsibility. Herbal use as an expression of resistance to control by large market, government, and political forces is one of the factors in their being a target of suppression by those powers. Herbs possess intrinsic democratic appeal since many are freely available weeds. Suppression of their use throughout history is legendary, from the burning of witches in the Middle Ages to the present. Big Pharma controls patents on engineered or chemically created substances that often mimic "active" plant fractions such as digitalis, reserpine, and morphine. Formerly those substances came from naturally occurring plant, animal and mineral sources available to all people. Now behemoth forces have found a new name for an old game.

Control of naturally occurring resources is not new. In the last four years, however, it has become particularly ponderous. The robber barons of the 19th and 20th century were superseded by the military-industrial complex of the mid-20th century. Even that has been trumped by the multinational corporate marriage with big government and media conglomerates to control ownership and quality of air, water, land and natural resources and information about their plunder.

In Robert Kennedy Jr.'s book, _Crimes Against Nature_, he defines fascism from the _American Heritage Dictionary_ as "a system of government that exercises a dictatorship of the extreme right, typically through the merging of state and business leadership together with belligerent nationalism."

Add to this the dumbing down of the educational system and the intimidation of local media by Big Media. Industry advertisers control major sources of information via TV, radio, and newsprint. Superimpose the government regulators who are hand selected by industry and you have a typical scenario of the "fox guarding the henhouse." Lobbyists for industry have seemingly unlimited money to buy politicians.

So where do herbs fit into this picture? I return to a basic personal belief that we are in charge of how we feel and what is good and wholesome for our families and ourselves. Begin at home with growing your own herbs—the ones you love the best--and use them to keep your family and yourself strong. Furthermore, grow some of your own organic food or support local producers who do through CSAs, farmers' markets, and stores that sell organic produce and animal products. If you really want to be on the cutting edge of this movement against the current version of fascism, keep a few chickens in your backyard and produce your own eggs.

Most importantly, **VOTE**. Yours does count!

"Begin at home with growing your own herbs—the ones you love the best—and use them to keep your family and yourself strong."

Benedictine Formula List, April 2021

Formulas	Benefit
Adaptogen Plus	Immune Health
Albizia & Passion Flower	Relaxation and Restful Sleep
Albizia	Relaxation & Calm
Anti-Fungal Oil	Anti-Microbial
Aletris	Menstrual & Digestion
Anti-Fungal Oil	Skin & Nail Issues
Anti-Fungal Tincture	Anti-Microbial
Anti-X	Cold Flu Season, Promotes Healthy Sinus
Arnica Oil Plus	HealthyJoints and Soft Tissue
Ashwagandha	Vitality
Astragalus	Energy and Immunity
Bilberry	Nutrition for Eyes
Black Cohosh	Hormone Balance
Blessed Thistle	Hormone Balance
Blood Root Plus	Healthy Blood
Boo Boo Juice	Cuts and Scrapes
Bug Bane Oil	Insect Repellant
Butternut Bark	Occasional Constipation
Calendula Oil	Skin
Calendula Tincture	Immune Function
California Poppy	Promotes Restful Sleep
Cat's Claw	Immune System and Intestines
Chickweed Oil	Skin Irritations, Splinters
Chill Out	Relaxation
Chinese Cold & Flu	Cold Flu, Sore Throat
Cleavers	Kidney Bladder

75

Formulas	Benefit
Dan Shen	Heart Health
Dandelion	Liver-Gall Bladder Health
Deep Lung	Healthy Lungs
Deep Lung 3 in 1	Cold-Flu Magic
Diaper Rash Oil	Delicate Skin
Diarrhea Relief for Adults	Occasional Diarrhea
Diet Aid	Dieting Help
Echinacea	Immune
Elderberry Plus	Immune, Cough
Elderberry Plus with Eleuthero	Post Flu Support & Stamina
Elecampane	Lung Health
Eleutherococcus	Immune and Stamina
Feverfew	Headache; Blood Vessel Relaxation
Five Flower	Withdrawal
Fo-ti	Healthy Brain
Gentian	Appetite & Digestion
Ginkgo	Health Brain and Memory
Golden Seal Tincture	Antimicrobial
Gotu Kola	Healthy Brains, Veins & Skin
Guarana	Natural Caffeine
Gum Protector Plus	Gum Health
Hawthorn Berry in Brandy	Healthy Heart
Hawthorn Leaf & Flower	Healthy Heart
Hayfever Allergies	Seasonal Allergies
Healing Oil	Cuts and Scrapes
Healing Salve	Salve for Cuts and Scrapes

Formulas	Benefit
Heart Blood Spleen Tonic	Cardiovascular & Circulation
Heart Health Glo	Cardiovascular Health
Herbal Mineral Tonic	Mineral Supplement
High Blood Sugar Balance	Blood Glucose Homeostasis
Holiday Bitters	Digestion (great tasting)
Hormonal Acne Relief (Blue Vervain)	Healthy Skin
Horse Chestnut Tonic	Healthy Veins
Horsetail	Bones and Urinary System
Immune Plus	Immune Health
Joint Relief for Adults	Cartilage and Joint Function
Kava	Relaxation and Restful Sleep
Kidney Care	Healthy Kidney and Bladder
Kidney Yang Adrenal Tonic	Vitality
Lymph Oil	Lymph Health
Marshmallow	Lung Health
Mega Ginseng Plus	Energy and Stamina
Memory Tonic	Mental Function
Menopause Plus	Hormone Support
Milk Thistle	Liver
Mistletoe	Joint Pain
Mother's Milk	Lactation
Motherwort	Relaxation and Nervous System
Moxa Oil	Massage Oil, Circulation
Moxa Tincture	Digestion
Mullein Flower Oil	Earache

Formulas	Benefit
Nettles	Whole Body Support
Nettles & Milk Thistle	Allergies
Nipple Balm Oil	Nursing Mothers
No Burp	Digestion
Olive	Immune
Passion Flower	Relaxation and Restful Sleep
Pau D'Arco	Mental Clarity
Propolis	Immune Health
Prostate Health Plus	Prostate Health; Urination
Reishi	Immune Health
Rhodiola rosea	Immune / Adaptagen
Rose Geranium Oil	Massage Oil for Women
Saw Palmetto	Male Health
Sight Saver	Nutrition for Maturing Eyes
St. John's Wort Oil	Nerve Health
St. John's Wort Tincture	Moody Blues
Tummy Ease	Healthy Digestion
Turkey Tail	Immune Support
UP!	Liver Support
Usnea	Immune Function; Sore Throat
Uva Ursi	Kidney-Bladder
Vitex	Hormone Balance
Xiao Yao Plus	PMS & Healthy Mood
Yellow Dock	Iron Source
Yew	Breast Tenderness
Yoni Oil	Vaginal Moisturizer

Formulas for Kids	Benefit
Calm for Kids	Relaxation
Constipation Relief for Kids	Constipation
Daily Minerals for Kids	Mineral Supplement
Diarrhea Relief for Kids	Diarrhea
Echinacea for Kids	Lymph
Elderberry Plus for Kids	Cough and Immune
Immune Help for Kids	Immune
Kidney Care for Kids	Kidney-Bladder Support
Skin Care for Kids	Skin
Sniffles for Kids	Cold-Flu Magic
Teething Relief for Kids	Teething
Tummy Ease for Kids	Digestion

Pet Formulas	Benefit
LoveMyPet Constipation Relief	Constipation
LoveMyPet Daily Minerals	Mineral Supplement
LoveMyPet Diarrhea Relief	Diarrhea
LoveMyPet Immune Boost	Immune Support
LoveMyPet Joint Relief	Joint Support
LoveMyPet Kidney-Bladder Relief	Kidney-Bladder Support
LoveMyPet Skin Comfort	Skin Inflammation
LoveMyPet Sniffles	Cold-Flu Magic; runny eyes
LoveMyPet Stinky Ear Oil	Ear Hygiene
LoveMyPet Stress Relief	Relaxation
LoveMyPet Tummy Ease	Digestion

Made in the USA
Middletown, DE
28 April 2021

38188613R00049